WHY DID GOD CREATE ME

JOURNEY INTO IDENTIFICATION

WILLIAM HATFIELD

ISBN:
978-1-9992526-8-7

ACKNOWLEDGEMENTS

We are all on a journey through life! I want to thank all my family and friends who stand besides me and encourage me when times are tough.

I especially want to thank my aunt Viola for all her work in editing and preparing the manuscript of my first book for publishing. The knowledge she shared will help me to continue writing. Her confidence in me ignited a gift I never realized I had. God created me with many gifts and one of them is to be a writer. Thank you Jesus for your great love.

DEDICATION

I DEDICATE THIS BOOK TO THE THIRSTY AND HUNGRY SAINTS OF GOD THAT DESIRE AN INTIMACY WITH THE HOLY SPIRIT LIKE NO OTHER. MY PRAYER IS THAT YOU CAN FIND THIS JOURNEY AS A SOURCE OF ENCOURAGEMENT, STRENGTH AND POWER TO OVERCOME LIFE'S STRUGGLES AND WALK IN A GREATER SENSE OF FREEDOM AND RELATIONSHIP WITH THE HOLY SPIRIT AND ALL WITHIN YOUR SPHERE OF INFLUENCE

PROLOGUE

EVERYBODY IS INTERESTED IN THE FUTURE. QUESTIONS ARE ASKED AND INTERNALIZED, MEDITATED ON AND DEPENDING ON THE OUTCOME OF THE MEDITATION, REACTION RESULTS. OUR REACTIONS ARE EITHER FEAR BASED OR FAITH BASED DEPENDING ON THE SUBJECT MEDITATED ON. KNOWING WHY GOD CREATED US AND OUR PURPOSE IN LIFE HELPS US TO WALK INTO FUTURE EVENTS WITH FAITH AND CONFIDENCE

CONTENTS

vi

1 Why did God create you Pg#7

2 The first wrong choice Pg#16

3 Paid in full Pg#36

4 Crises Pg#58

5 Transformation Pg#61

6 Changing nature's Pg#91

7 Your calling Pg#110

8 Epilogue Pg#121

9 About the Author Pg#122

1 **Why Did God Create You?**

Why Did God Create You?
What we have seen and [ourselves] heard we are also telling you, so that you too may realize and enjoy fellowship as partners and partakers with us. And [this] fellowship that we have (which is a distinguishing mark of Christians) is with the Father and with His Son Jesus Christ, the Messiah. - 1 John 1:3

We see in the beginning God created mankind. **Genesis 1:26** KJV: And God said, Let us make man in our image, after our likeness: and let them have dominion over the fish of the sea, and over the fowl of the air, and over the cattle, and over all the earth, and over every creeping thing that creepeth upon the earth.

God created man in His image and likeness. Go look in the mirror and realize you look like God.

Image

['imij]

NOUN

1. A representation of the external form of a person or thing in art.
    "Her work juxtaposed images from serious and popular art"
    Synonyms:
    Likeness · resemblance · depiction · portra
    yal · representation · statue · statuette · sc
    ulpture · bust · effigy · figure · figurine ·
    Doll · carving · painting · picture · portrait ·
     drawing · sketch ·
    Artist's impression

2. The general impression that a person, organization, or product presents to the public.
    "She strives to project an image of youth"
    Synonyms:
    Public perception · public
    conception · public
    impression · persona · profile · face ·

identity · front · facade · mask · guise · role · part · portrayal · depiction

3.   A simile or metaphor.

"He uses the image of a hole to describe emotional emptiness"

Synonyms:

simile · metaphor · metonymy · figure of speech · trope · figurative expression · turn of phrase · rhetorical device · conceit · word painting · word picture

VERB

1.   make a representation of the external form of.

"artworks that imaged women's bodies"

When you study the meaning of image you see a lot of meanings, resemblance for example is a term people use to say you look like one of your parents. Facial expressions body shape and even attitudes resemble or remind people of parents. Since we are the children of God shouldn't our entire being be a resemblance or reminder to others of our Father God.

portrayal

[ˌpôrˈtrā(ə)l]

NOUN

1.   a depiction of someone or something in a work of art or literature.
"a realistic portrayal of war"
synonyms:
painting · picture · drawing · portrait · sketch · representation · depiction · study · rendering · artist's impression · characterization · description · delineation · presentation · evocation · performance as · acting · playing · enacting · interpretation · personation

- a description of someone or something in a particular way; a representation.
"the media portrayal of immigration"
- an instance of an actor playing a part in a movie or play; a performance.

"his portrayal of the title character"
Portrayal one of the meanings of image is an intense thought. Every part of our lives character, actions, personalities are to paint a picture and representation of God. We are to leave an impression of God's nature and goodness on all within the sphere of our influence.

likeness

['līknəs]

NOUN

1. the fact or quality of being alike; resemblance.

   "her likeness to him was astonishing" · "a family likeness can be seen among all the boys"

   synonyms:

   resemblance · similarity · alikeness · samen ess · similitude ·
   congruity · affinity · correspondence · anal ogy · parallelism · agreement · relationship · identity · identicalness · uniformity ·

conformity · equivalence
- 　　　the semblance, guise, or outward appearance of.
"humans are described as being made in God's likeness"
synonyms:
semblance · guise · appearance · outward form · form · shape · image · aspect · character · mien
- 　　　a portrait or representation.
"the only known likeness of Dorothy as a young woman"
synonyms:
representation · image · depiction · portr ayal · delineation ·
profile · picture · drawing · sketch · artist's
impression · painting · portrait · photogra ph · study · bust ·
statue · statuette · sculpture · icon

One of the meanings of likeness is photograph, in other words mankind looks just like God. Not only do we look like God but our actions and attitudes are supposed to be similar and the same as God. God created mankind in His own class.

Little Lower Than God

Yet You have made him but a little lower than God [or heavenly beings], and You have crowned him with glory and honour. **Psalm 8:5 (AMPC)**

Our verse today says God made mankind a little lower than Himself.

In some translations, it says we were made a little lower than the angels. But the word "angels" was translated from the Hebrew word Elohim, which is the very same word used in Genesis 1:1, "In the beginning God [Elohim] created the heavens and the earth."

Here God is saying we were created a little lower than Him, not angels. According to Hebrews 1:14, angels are our servants, commissioned to protect and minister to us.

Not only did God create us to be just a little lower than Him, but He also crowned us with glory and honour. **You have dignity and worth in His eyes. Do you realize it?**

God made the earth for mankind. He decorated it with gorgeous plants and scenery, but it's all for His crowning creation: mankind.

God gave us dominion over animals, and we are to take care of them— but we're not one of them. We are not just some evolved breed of chimpanzees, even though our DNA is similar. In fact, our DNA could be identical and it wouldn't make one bit of difference. We are who we are because we have a spirit within us! That's the real you! Your body is just your earth-suit, designed to house your spirit.

When we begin to believe that we're just one of the animals, just a few percent away from the DNA of a chimpanzee, evolved from single celled organisms over millions of years, it destroys our sense of self-worth.

We were created magnificently and intentionally. We are loved infinitely and we have purpose! https://leonfontaine.com/little-lower-than-god/

God created mankind in His class to have fellowship with him on His level. Not only to fellowship on His level but to love on His level. We were not created as robots or clones to do and say things automatically. We were created with a free will and the right and power to make choices. God knew the risks of creating mankind with free will and the power to make choices, they could choose wrong and did. Choosing wrong brought about consequences that brought death and destruction to mankind. God created mankind to know righteousness only, never to know and experience evil.

2 THE FIRST WRONG CHOICE

The Garden of Eden

1Thus the heavens and the earth, and all the host of them, were finished. **2**And on the seventh day God ended His work which He had done, and He rested on the seventh day from all His work which He had done. **3**Then God blessed the seventh day and sanctified it, because in it He rested from all His work which God had created and made.

4This *is* the history of the heavens and the earth when they were created, in the day that the LORD God made the earth and the heavens, **5**before any plant of the field was in the earth and before any herb of the field had grown. For the LORD God had not caused it to rain on the earth, and *there was* no man to till the ground; **6**but a mist went up from the earth and watered the whole face of the ground.

7And the LORD God formed man *of* the dust of the ground, and breathed into his nostrils the breath of life; and man became a living being.

Life in God's Garden

8The LORD God planted a garden eastward in Eden, and there He put the man whom He had formed. **9**And out of the ground the LORD God made every tree grow that is pleasant to the sight and good for food. The tree of life *was* also in the midst of the garden, and the tree of the knowledge of good and evil.

10Now a river went out of Eden to water the garden, and from there it parted and became four riverheads. **11**The name of the first *is* Pishon; it *is* the one which skirts the whole land of Havilah, where *there is* gold. **12**And the gold of that land *is* good. Bdellium and the onyx stone *are* there. **13**The name of the second river *is* Gihon; it *is* the one which goes around the whole land of Cush. **14**The name of the third river *is* Hiddekel;__it *is* the one which goes toward the east of Assyria. The fourth river *is* the Euphrates.

15Then the LORD God took the man and put him in the garden of Eden to tend and keep it. **16And the LORD God commanded the man, saying, "Of every tree of the garden you may freely eat; 17but of the tree of the knowledge of good and evil you shall not eat, for in the day that you eat of it you shall surely die."**

18And the LORD God said, "*It is* not good that man should be alone; I will make him a helper comparable to him." **19**Out of the ground the LORD God formed every beast of the field and every bird of the air, and brought *them* to Adam to see what he would call them. And whatever Adam called each living creature, that *was* its name. **20**So Adam gave names to all cattle, to the birds of the air, and to every beast of the field. But for Adam there was not found a helper comparable to him.

21And the LORD God caused a deep sleep to fall on Adam, and he slept; and He took one of his ribs, and closed up the flesh in its place. **22**Then the rib which the LORD God had taken from man He made into a woman, and He brought her to the man.

23And Adam said:

"This *is* now bone of my bones
And flesh of my flesh;
She shall be called Woman,
Because she was taken out

of Man."

24Therefore a man shall leave his father and mother and be joined to his wife, and they shall become one flesh.

25And they were both naked, the man and his wife, and were not ashamed.

God gave man an abundance to enjoy and only one restriction. **16And the Lord God commanded the man, saying, "Of every tree of the garden you may freely eat; 17but of the tree of the knowledge of good and evil you shall not eat, for in the day that you eat of it you shall surely die."**

The restriction wasn't meant to rob Adam and Eve of goodness and pleasure but to protect them. I personally believe that God would eventually teach them about good and evil. Being new creations to me suggests limitations like a new born baby. The new born baby has great potential and increases their abilities as they grow and develop. Eventually the child enters adulthood and you see them working at a much greater capacity than when being a youth. I believe this was the same thing for Adam and Eve.

You look at what Adam and Eve were given them upon their creation. Genesis 1:[26] Then God said, "Let Us make man in Our image, according to Our likeness; let them have dominion over the fish of the sea, over the birds of the air, and over the cattle, over all the earth and over every creeping thing that creeps on the earth." [27] So God created man in His *own* image; in the image of God He created him; male and female He created them. [28] Then God blessed them, and God said to them, "Be fruitful and multiply; fill the earth and subdue it; have dominion over the fish of the sea, over the birds of the air, and over every living thing that moves on the earth."

Adam and Eve were given authority and dominion over a planet and all creatures on that planet. Adam was not a dumb cave man but had supernatural intelligence and knowledge. Genesis **2: 19 Out of the ground the LORD God formed every beast of the field and every bird of the air, and brought *them* to Adam to see what he would call them. And whatever Adam called each living creature, that *was* its name. 20 So Adam gave names to all cattle, to the birds of the air, and to every beast of the field.**

I think they were given more than enough at creation to keep them busy for a long time; Authority and dominion over a planet and all creatures that dwelt upon it; and supernatural knowledge and understanding. In Genesis three you will notice Eve wasn't amazed or freaked out when the serpent talked to her audible. It was like oh yeah life goes on, wonder what the blue jays have to say today.

Genesis 3

New King James Version

The Temptation and Fall of Man

1Now the serpent was more cunning than any beast of the field which the LORD God had made. And he said to the woman, "Has God indeed said, 'You shall not eat of every tree of the garden'?"

2And the woman said to the serpent, "We may eat the fruit of the trees of the garden; **3**but of the fruit of the tree which *is* in the midst of the garden,

God has said, 'You shall not eat it, nor shall you touch it, lest you die.' "

4Then the serpent said to the woman, "You will not surely die. **5**For God knows that in the day you eat of it your eyes will be opened, and you will be like God, knowing good and evil."

6So when the woman saw that the tree *was* good for food, that it *was* pleasant to the eyes, and a tree desirable to make *one* wise, she took of its fruit and ate. She also gave to her husband with her, and he ate. **7**Then the eyes of both of them were opened, and they knew that they *were* naked; and they sewed fig leaves together and made themselves coverings. **8**And they heard the sound of the LORD God walking in the garden in the cool of the day, and Adam and his wife hid themselves from the presence of the LORD God among the trees of the garden.

9Then the Lord God called to Adam and said to him, "Where *are* you?"

10So he said, "I heard Your voice in the garden, and I was afraid because I was naked; and I hid myself."

11And He said, "Who told you that you *were* naked? Have you eaten from the tree of which I commanded you that you should not eat?"

12Then the man said, "The woman whom You gave *to be* with me, she gave me of the tree, and I ate."

13And the Lord God said to the woman, "What *is* this you have done?"

The woman said, "The serpent deceived me, and I ate."

14So the Lord God said to the serpent:

"Because you have done this,
You *are* cursed more than all
cattle, And more than every

beast of the field;
On your belly you shall go, And
you shall eat dust
All the days of your life.
15And I will put enmity Between
you and the woman,
And between your seed and her
Seed; He shall bruise your head,
And you shall bruise His heel.”

16To the woman He said:

“I will greatly multiply your
sorrow and your conception;
In pain you shall bring forth
children; Your desire *shall be* for
your husband,
And he shall rule over you.”

17Then to Adam He said, “Because you
have heeded the voice of your wife,
and have eaten from the tree of which
I commanded you, saying, ‘You shall
not eat of it’:

"Cursed *is* the ground for your
sake;
In toil you shall eat *of* it
All the days of your life.
18Both thorns and thistles it
shall bring forth for you,
And you shall eat the herb of the
field.
19In the sweat of your face you
shall eat bread
Till you return to the ground,
For out of it you were taken;
For dust you *are,*
And to dust you shall return."

20And Adam called his wife's name
Eve, because she was the mother of all
living.

21Also for Adam and his wife
the LORD God made tunics of skin, and
clothed them.

22Then the LORD God said, "Behold,
the man has become like one of Us, to

know good and evil. And now, lest he put out his hand and take also of the tree of life, and eat, and live forever" — **23**therefore the LORD God sent him out of the garden of Eden to till the ground from which he was taken. **24**So He drove out the man; and He placed cherubim at the east of the garden of Eden, and a flaming sword which turned every way, to guard the way to the tree of life.

Notice the woman fell for the temptation of the serpent but the man made a choice. Adam knew God before he met Eve, Adam made the choice to go with Eve rather than stay with God. We have two situations to deal with deception on the woman's part and outright rebellion on the man's part. They chose to obey Satan thus relinquishing their authority over the earth to Satan who is now known as God of this world. Not only losing their authority to a fallen angel they partook of Satan's nature as well. Satan or Lucifer as he is known as well rebelled against God in heaven and deceived a third of the angels to follow him in his rebellion. Their attempt failed and got them cast out of heaven.

Now mankind is in an interesting predicament they have now received a sin nature from Satan and since everything born from their union will be born with that sin nature as well. The wages of sin is eternal separation from God and go to the place created for Lucifer and the fallen angels a lake of fire where the torment never ends for all eternity.

Take a good look at how people react in the earth, they do things they think will benefit them without really knowing the consequences of their actions. They hope their decisions bring them pie in the sky and blue jays singing their praises. Then there is I will do things my way regardless how it affects others as long as I benefit from it. Mankind is in a bad situation and the sad thing is; mankind created the situation and only mankind can fix the problem.

God in his great love and value for mankind decided to fix the problem mankind's wrong choices creates.

Romans 5

New King James Version

Faith Triumphs in Trouble

1Therefore, having been justified by faith, we have peace with God through our Lord Jesus Christ, **2**through whom also we have access by faith into this grace in which we stand, and rejoice in hope of the glory of God. **3**And not only *that,* but we also glory in tribulations, knowing that tribulation produces perseverance; **4**and perseverance, character; and character, hope. **5**Now hope does not disappoint, because the love of God has been poured out in our hearts by the Holy Spirit who was given to us.

Christ in Our Place

6For when we were still without strength, in due time Christ died for the ungodly. **7**For scarcely for a righteous man will one die; yet perhaps for a good man someone would even dare to die. **8**But God demonstrates His own love toward us, in that while we were still sinners, Christ died for us. **9**Much more then, having now been justified by His blood, we shall be saved from wrath through

Him. **10**For if when we were enemies we were reconciled to God through the death of His Son, much more, having been reconciled, we shall be saved by His life. **11**And not only *that,* but we also rejoice in God through our Lord Jesus Christ, through whom we have now received the reconciliation.

Death in Adam, Life in Christ

12Therefore, just as through one man sin entered the world, and death through sin, and thus death spread to all men, because all sinned— **13**(For until the law sin was in the world, but sin is not imputed when there is no law. **14**Nevertheless death reigned from Adam to Moses, even over those who had not sinned according to the likeness of the transgression of Adam, who is a type of Him who was to come. **15**But the free gift *is* not like the offense. For if by the one man's offense many died, much more the grace of God and the gift by the grace of the one Man, Jesus Christ, abounded too many. **16**And the gift *is* not like *that which came* through the one who sinned. For the judgment *which came* from one *offense resulted* in condemnation, but the free gift *which came* from many offenses *resulted* in justification. **17**For if by the one man's offense death reigned through the one, much more those who receive abundance of grace and of the gift of righteousness will reign in life through the One, Jesus Christ.)

18Therefore, as through one man's offense *judgment came* to all men, resulting in condemnation, even so through one Man's righteous act *the free gift came* to all men, resulting in justification of life. **19**For as by one man's disobedience many were made sinners, so also by one Man's obedience many will be made righteous.

20Moreover the law entered that the offense might abound. But where sin abounded, grace abounded much more, **21**so that as sin reigned in death, even so grace might reign through righteousness to eternal life through Jesus Christ our Lord.

Jesus Christ had to come into the earth as a man born of a woman to have legal access into the earth.

"WHEN GOD SENT HIS SON!"

TEXT: Galatians 4:4-7 (NKJV)

But when the fullness of the time had come, God sent forth His Son, born of a woman, born under the law, to redeem those who were under the law, that we might receive the adoption as sons. And because you are sons, God has sent forth the Spirit of

His Son into your hearts, crying out,
"Abba, Father!" Therefore you are no
longer a slave but a son, and if a son,
then an heir of God through Christ."

3 PAID IN FULL

If one contemplates it, even for a few moments, a truth about our faith stands out as something truly remarkable. The Creator of all things, the Ever-Living One, became flesh and blood just like us and died to pay for our sins. His sacrifice was prophesied to our first parents (Genesis 3:15). And it is pictured by Passover, the very first of the seven Festivals God uses to explain His plan of salvation (1 Corinthians 5:7).

The price paid on our behalf, to remove our sins, should highlight to us the truly terrible nature of sin. Our Father wants us to fully and deeply understand the connection between sin and its consequences. Jesus Christ led a pure and sinless life—a life of loving obedience and unwavering devotion to God—and it is not a stretch of the imagination to believe that one factor in that feat was the Savior's perfect understanding of the terrible price sin exacts of the sinner. He had to know that price, because it is a price He had committed from the foundation of the world to pay in full (Revelation 13:8).

When we consider carefully the final events of the last Passover of Jesus' earthly ministry, almost two millennia ago, we see displayed multiple elements of the price of sin. And we see a Savior who was willing to pay the full price for those He loved.

Let's take some time to review three of those elements and their reflection in Jesus' sacrifice, and let's seek to come closer to God's own perspective on the consequences of sin.

Sin Causes Death

Death is the most obvious consequence of sin that many associate with Jesus Christ's sacrifice. And Scripture is certainly clear about it.

Romans 6:23 declares that "the wages of sin is death, but the gift of God is eternal life in Christ Jesus our Lord." And those wages have been earned by each and every one of us (Romans 3:23). Death is a natural consequence of sin. The Lord's brother, James, details very plainly the pathway we tread to sin: "But each one is tempted when he is drawn away by his own desires and enticed. Then, when desire has conceived, it gives birth to sin; and sin, when it is full-grown, brings forth death" (James 1:14–15). It is not sin to be tempted—even Jesus Christ faced temptation (Hebrews 4:15). That is part of what makes Him our compassionate High Priest. But He did not entertain the thoughts that temptation engenders.

Had He, even once in His 33½ years of life, committed a single sin, then He, too, would have earned death.

But His death was to be reserved to pay our debt, not His own.

Jesus Christ, the most innocent Man ever to walk the earth, was nailed to a piece of wood—crucified like a despised and hated criminal—and died. While most modern translations make the exact events less obvious than they should be, an accurate account of His death is supported by some of the oldest extant copies of the New Testament. Motivated by unknown reasons, but certainly in fulfillment of prophecy, a Roman soldier approached the Son of God—already hanging helpless and in agony—and rammed a spear into His exposed side (John 19:34), spilling His blood and fulfilling what was predicted of Him (vv. 35–37). Upon being stabbed, He cried out with a loud voice and died (Matthew 27:50; Mark 15:37; Luke 23:46).

And it is important. In Hebrews we learn that it is only through the spilling of Jesus' blood—shed for us—that remission of our sins is possible (Hebrews 9:12–14, 22).

But what does this price Jesus was willing to pay teach us about the price of sin?

The profound and unalterable connection between sin and death is easy for us to miss in our day-to-day lives. When sin presents itself as an option, it is usually quite tempting. Even God's word affirms that the choice to sin can bring momentary pleasure and satisfaction—can feel right—though it is pleasure that, ultimately, does not last (Hebrews 11:25).

When making a choice to sin, we are choosing death over life, however deceptively it may be disguised. Solomon tries to make such a connection in the Proverbs, for example, explaining that the home of an immoral seductress promises to be a source of pleasure and delight, but it is quite the opposite. "For her house leads down to death, and her paths to the dead"

(Proverbs 2:18). Who would go to the dwelling of a loose woman if they saw adultery and fornication as God does and perceived her home as one filled with corpses?

The price Jesus paid by sacrificing His own life for our sins makes that connection between death and sin very clear. It demands that we recognize the truth that the only death significant enough to free us from the debt we owe was the death of our own Eternal Creator. All other payments would fall short. Only the death of the Ever-Living One was sufficient to pay the price for the sins of all mankind and redeem us from the fate we earned.

The Eternal had to die like the finite, that the finite might have the opportunity to live for eternity. No other payment would suffice to remove the curse that our sins have brought upon us. And He was willing to pay that price.

Sin Causes Physical Suffering, Sickness and Broken Bodies

But Christ's death was more than simply a cessation of life. In the United States, convicts who have been sentenced to death are executed in a manner designed to reflect inherent human dignity and avoid being "cruel and unusual." Most commonly today, the prisoner is given a sequence of chemical injections designed to first render him unconscious, then to paralyze his muscles so that no spasmodic movements diminish the dignity of his death, and then to stop his heart.

Such a respectfully managed death was the exact opposite of what Jesus Christ experienced.

The Scriptures make clear that first His body was brutally and painfully broken for us. Explaining the symbol of the bread at the Passover the night before He died, Jesus said to His disciples, "Take, eat; this is My body which is broken for you" (1 Corinthians 11:24). And His body was broken, indeed. Pontius Pilate had Jesus Christ scourged before His crucifixion (Matthew 27:26; Mark 15:15; John 19:1).

Roman scourging was a horrific practice, in which a person—generally with his hands tied above his head and stripped, exposing his body—was whipped by one or two *lictors*. The whipping instrument was usually a specially designed leather whip of multiple strips of varied lengths, in which were embedded small iron balls or sharp pieces of animal bone that would tear and rip at the flesh. In its famous 1986 publication, "On the Physical Death of Jesus Christ," the *Journal of the American Medical Association* described the scourging from a physiological point of view:

As the Roman soldiers repeatedly struck the victim's back with full force, the iron balls would cause deep contusions, and the leather thongs and sheep bones would cut into the skin and subcutaneous tissues. Then, as the flogging continued, the lacerations would tear into the underlying skeletal muscles and produce quivering ribbons of bleeding flesh. Pain and blood loss generally set the stage for circulatory shock (JAMA, March 21, 1986, Vol 255, No. 11).

Such a terrible treatment calls to mind the prophecy that "His visage was marred more than any man, and His form more than the sons of men" (Isaiah 52:14).

In addition, we are told that a garrison of Roman soldiers created a crown of thorns for Him to wear, spat on Him and beat Him in the head with a reed (Matthew 27:29–30; Mark 15:16–19).

If Christ's death was the only goal, why did it have to be a brutal death involving the mutilation of His body?

There are a number of benefits we, as His people, gain from His willingness to experience such horrors. For instance, when we ourselves suffer, we can look to Him who went through great suffering so faithfully, and find encouragement to face our own trials. One of the keys to suffering in this world with faith intact is to recognize that our Creator was willing, Himself, to become flesh and blood and personally experience suffering—to share in our severe trials with us, so that we might share eternity with Him.

However, Scripture records a very specific role that Christ's stripes, cuts, wounds and bruises serve, described by the Apostle Peter. In his first letter, he speaks of the Messiah "who Himself bore our sins in His own body on the tree, that we, having died to sins, might live for righteousness—by whose stripes you were healed" (1 Peter 2:24). Here, the Apostle is referring to the messianic prophecy of Isaiah 53:5, which says that "He was wounded for our transgressions, He was bruised for our iniquities; the chastisement for our peace was upon Him, and by His stripes we are healed."

How does this price Jesus paid relate to sin?

Take the time to reflect: What is the source of sickness? Disease? Injury? Infirmities?

Such physical afflictions are present in the world due to sin. It is part of the price that is paid for a world in which sin is a frequently chosen option. God speaks of diseases and afflictions as being part of what comes on a people who reject their Creator's commands (Deuteronomy 28:27, 60), and He similarly associates obeying Him with freedom from sickness and with healing (Exodus 23:25). He declares Himself the God "who forgives all your iniquities, who heals all your diseases" (Psalm 103:3). In James' instruction to request anointing from the elders of the

Church when we are sick, there is a connection suggested between illness and sin: "Is anyone among you sick? Let him call for the elders of the church, and let them pray over him, anointing him with oil in the name of the Lord. And the prayer of faith will save the sick, and the Lord will raise him up. And if he has committed sins, he will be forgiven" (James 5:14–15).

This does not mean that we are always the ones who have sinned when we become ill—after all, if a sick co-worker ignores the biblical principle of quarantine (e.g., Numbers 19:13, 20), we may become sick, too! But the cause is still sin. (See also John 9:2–3.)

God did not create a world destined to be infected with disease, sickness and disability. Such conditions in our world are the result of the presence of sin. Broken bodies are part of the price we pay in this world for sin. And Jesus bore *that* price on Himself as well, in His own broken body. He

Himself broke none of the laws of God that are meant to protect our health. He ate no unclean thing. He would have treated His body with the respect God expects (cf. 1 Corinthians 6:19). The gluttony and abuse of drink and other substances that destroy our bodies would have been foreign to Him. And yet His body was broken beyond what most of us can even imagine.

Why?

As we read earlier from Peter: It is by His stripes that we are healed (1 Peter 2:24). This physical price that is exacted by sin, He paid in full, as well.

God has our salvation in mind—with glorious bodies that will last forever—and these relatively few years we now live in these temporary dwellings here on earth (2 Corinthians 5:1–4) are training and preparation for that eternal good.

But this does not take away from the fact that Christ's broken body does thoroughly reflect the consequences of sin that manifest in our flesh and that it represents an important part of the price He paid. Paul told the Corinthians at the Passover season, "many are weak and sick among you, and many sleep [have died]" due to a failure to eat and drink of the Passover bread and wine in a worthy manner. Among the unworthy elements he identifies? They were "not discerning the Lord's body" (1 Corinthians 11:29–30).

It is interesting that the Old Testament, as well, describes individuals in need of physical healing due to keeping the Passover in a manner unworthy for the times (2 Chronicles 30:18–20).

Jesus Christ did not deserve to have His body ravaged. But ravaged it was. He was willing to pay that price.

Sin Causes Separation from God

A third unavoidable cost associated with sin is separation from God. It is expressed, perhaps, most simply in Isaiah 59, where the prophet warns the house of Jacob, "Behold, the Lord's hand is not shortened, that it cannot save; nor His ear heavy, that it cannot hear. But your iniquities have separated you from your God; and your sins have hidden His face from you, so that He will not hear" (vv. 1–2).

If we refuse to separate ourselves from sin, sin separates us from God.

The purity and holiness of God is clearly and unmistakably taught throughout Scripture. Psalm 5:4 tells us that God will not dwell alongside evil, and after fire struck down Nadab and Abihu, the sons of Aaron, for their disregard of His holiness, He warned, "By those who come near Me I must be regarded as holy" (Leviticus 10:3).

We are assured that, at the completion of His plan for mankind's salvation, He will ensure that His glorious Kingdom and Family are forever separated from evil (Revelation 22:15). He dwells in "unapproachable light" (1 Timothy 6:16), and there is no place for wickedness and unrighteousness—sin—in His presence.

Again, in the words of Isaiah, our sins separate us from God. It is part of the price.

And Jesus Christ paid that price, as well.

While hanging there, crucified like a criminal for our sins and not His own, the Savior cried out loudly, *"Eloi, Eloi, lama sabachthani?"* which Mark 15:34 tells us is translated, "My God, My God, why have You forsaken Me?" Jesus was quoting Psalm 22: "My God, My God, why have You forsaken Me? Why are You so far from helping Me, and from the words of My groaning?" (v. 1).

We need not presume that Christ was in confusion as to why He was in such a state, but His cry does reveal the burden of that state: He was, at that point, forsaken by God.

It was not that He was not loved by the Father—the One who had known and loved Him from eternity past, in a relationship of intimacy and trust that we mere mortals can scarcely imagine. He was loved dearly. But that distance in that moment was part of the plan. For that distance is part of the price of sin.

Some theologians have resisted the idea that God would abandon Jesus in that moment, saying that it removes from us the confidence we should have that God would never abandon *us*, with an eye to the promise He will never leave us and never forsake us (Hebrews 13:5). However, they miss the point. We can trust that promise *all the more* because Jesus Christ paid that part of the price of sin.

On this point, the Apostle Paul uses clarity of words that offend many, but which are true nonetheless: "For He [God] made Him [Christ] who knew no sin to *be sin for us*, that we might become the righteousness of God in Him" (2 Corinthians 5:21). I believe Christ actually became sin not just a representation of sin. But at that moment, on that stake of torture and death, Jesus Christ became all of our sins. And because sin separates from God, that separation became yet one more aspect of *our* penalty that the Son of God willingly bore for us, so that those who turn to God need not bear it themselves. By becoming our sin we become Christ's righteousness. If we have righteousness we could lose it, we are righteousness and sealed never to lose it.

Paul explains in Galatians 3:13 that Christ became a curse on our behalf, taking our curse upon Himself, since "Cursed is everyone who hangs on a tree." Paul was referring to Deuteronomy 21:23, which says of those who are put to death and hanged on a tree that "he who is hanged is accursed of God."

Jesus Christ did nothing to deserve being accursed. He did nothing to deserve separation from God. The profound loneliness He bore in those final moments of His suffering—when He no longer felt the presence of the One He had never been without—was a loneliness He did not earn. We earn it. Our sins separate *us* from God. It is part of the price, and He took on that price willingly so that those who turn to Him need never have to suffer that price, themselves.

Paid in Full

We don't always appreciate the price that sin exacts. But in His final moments during the last Passover of His earthly life, Jesus Christ illustrated the terrible fullness of that cost. Sin earns for us nothing but death. It destroys us physically. And it separates us from our Creator.

Yet the Son of God faced those consequences and willingly paid in full the price exacted by sin. He did so in order to open the door for us to an eternal future in His Family, in which we will never know sin again. Instead of death, we can enjoy eternal, unending *life* (John 3:16). Instead of the suffering of sick and broken bodies, we can access healing in this life and, ultimately, enjoy bodies of power and glory that will never know pain (1 Corinthians 15:42–44; Revelation 21:4). And instead of separation, we can enjoy dwelling in God's loving family, alongside Him forever (Revelation 21:3).

For those willing to repent, turn aside from sin and turn toward their Creator, there remains the opportunity to experience the joy of knowing the debt of their sins has been *completely removed*. Because that

Creator, Jesus Christ, was willing to pay the price of sin—and to pay it in full.

https://www.lcg.org/lcn/2018/march-april/paid-full-completeness-price-christ-paid

Jesus Christ paid a heavy price to restore us into fellowship with the trinity. We now have access to God the Father through the Holy Spirit because of the shed blood of Jesus at the cross. We receive Jesus as our savior and are born again children of God. We're born of God, we receive His divine, eternal life in our spirit, and we become His children. Our **human spirit** is the unique place for God's Spirit to enter into us to make us His children, and it is also the place from which He goes on to fill our entire being.

Galatians 4:19 my little children, for whom I labor in birth again until Christ is formed in you,

When we accept Jesus our spirits are made perfect but our soul's need to be worked on. I believe the apostle Paul in the chapter above is referring to this situation of Christ formed in us. Romans 12:1–2 I appeal to you therefore, brothers, by the mercies of God, to present your bodies as a living sacrifice, holy and acceptable to God, which is your spiritual worship. Do not be conformed to this world, but be transformed by the renewal of your mind, that by testing you may discern what is the will of God, what is good and acceptable and perfect.

By continually renewing our minds we enter into a deeper fellowship with the Holy Spirit and we can discern God from the spirit of the world.

4 CRISES

When crisis comes people naturally respond in fear. Some great fear called worry and anxiety others a little fear or simple concern. Bottom line is fear has its roots in you to grow deep and bring destruction. With this current pandemic called covid19 the world is going into exaggerated fear, claiming death's that are because of something else as this virus death. Exaggerating the numbers gives the virus more power than it has.

That's the way of the world being under the sway of the wicked one, Lucifer. 1 John 5:19 we know that we are of God, and the whole world

lies **under the sway of the wicked one**. How is the world under the sway of the wicked one? Basically, through our five physical senses. Seeing, hearing, smelling, touching,

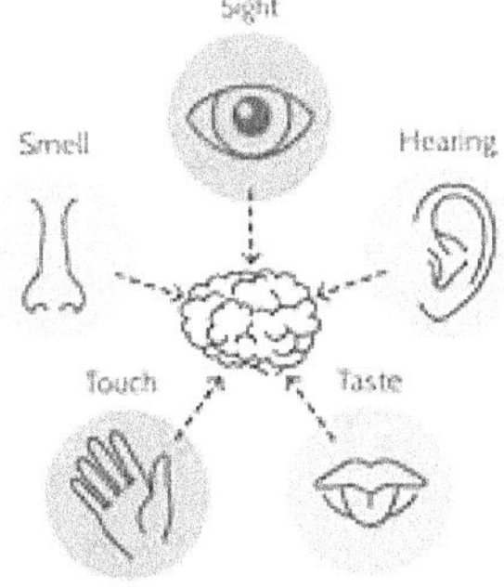

and tasting.

There is an organization that takes advantage of our senses and does its best to condition us to believe its agenda. This organization is called the news media. It is supposed to report the news but it in turn creates news stories through subterfuge and manipulation of facts. Nevertheless it is what it is. This world under the sway of the wicked one has one agenda and that agenda is fear and destruction of the human race. Satan, the thief has an agenda for the human race. **John 10:10** [10]The thief comes only to steal and kill and destroy; I have come that they may have life, and have it to the full. As born again bible believers and doers of the Word of God we have a different agenda to fulfill. The agenda for born again Christians is not to be molded into the image of the world but to be transformed into the image of Christ.

5 **TRANSFORMATION**

2 Peter 1:1-21

1Simon Peter, a servant and an apostle of Jesus Christ, to them that have obtained like precious faith with us through the righteousness of God and our Saviour Jesus Christ:

2Grace and peace be multiplied unto you through the knowledge of God, and of Jesus our Lord,

3According as his divine power hath given unto us all things that *pertain* unto life and godliness, through the knowledge of him that hath called us to glory and virtue:

4Whereby are given unto us exceeding great and precious promises: that by these ye might be partakers of the divine nature, having escaped the corruption that is in the world through lust.

5And beside this, giving all diligence, add to your faith virtue; and to virtue knowledge;

6And to knowledge temperance; and to temperance patience; and to patience godliness;

7And to godliness brotherly kindness; and to brotherly kindness charity.

8For if these things be in you, and abound, they make *you that ye*
shall neither *be* barren nor unfruitful in the knowledge of our Lord Jesus Christ.

9But he that lacketh these things is blind, and cannot see afar off, and hath forgotten that he was purged from his old sins.

10Wherefore the rather, brethren, give diligence to make your calling and election sure: for if ye do these things, ye shall never fall:

11For so an entrance shall be ministered unto you abundantly into the everlasting kingdom of our Lord and Saviour Jesus Christ.

12Wherefore I will not be negligent to put you always in remembrance of these things, though ye know *them,* and be established in the present truth.

13Yea, I think it meet, as long as I am in this tabernacle, to stir you up by putting *you* in remembrance;

14Knowing that shortly I must put off *this* my tabernacle, even as our Lord Jesus Christ hath shewed me.

15Moreover I will endeavour that ye may be able after my decease to have these things always in remembrance.

16For we have not followed cunningly devised fables, when we made known unto you the power and coming of our Lord Jesus Christ, but were eyewitnesses of his majesty.

17He received honor and glory from God the Father when the voice came to him from the Majestic Glory, saying, "This is my Son, whom I love; with him I am well pleased."

18And this voice which came from heaven we heard, when we were with him in the holy mount.

19We have also a more sure word of prophecy; whereunto ye do well that ye

take heed, as unto a light that shineth in a dark place, until the day dawn, and the day star arise in your hearts:

20Knowing this first, that no prophecy of the scripture is of any private interpretation.

21For the prophecy came not in old time by the will of man: but holy men of God spake *as they were* moved by the Holy Ghost.

This scripture is a golden nugget amidst a gold field (Word of God).

Verse 1 we have obtained precious faith through the righteousness of Jesus Christ. We didn't have to work for it or earn it in any way. **Ephesians 2:8-9** [8]For it is by grace you have been saved, through faith- and this is not from yourselves, it is the gift of God- [9]not by works, so that no one can boast. We receive salvation by choice. I may not know God or much about Him but I choose to believe the bible that He loves me and has a greater destiny for me than I can imagine.

Verse **2**Grace and peace be multiplied unto you through the knowledge of God, and of Jesus our Lord, Tells me that by my growing in the knowledge of God and Jesus our Lord I will receive grace and peace.

Grace

[grās]

NOUN

Grace (noun) · **graces** (plural noun) · **grace period** (noun) · **grace periods** (plural noun) · **His Grace** (noun) · **Her Grace** (noun) · **Your Grace** (noun) · **the Graces** (plural noun)

1.   Simple elegance or refinement of movement.

"She moved through the water with effortless grace"

Synonyms:

Elegance · stylishness · poise ·

finesse · charm · gracefulness · dexterity

· adroitness · deftness · fluidity of movement · fluency · flow · suppleness · smoothness · ease · effortlessness · naturalness · neatness · precision · agility · nimbleness · light-footedness · poetry in motion · flowingness · lightsomeness

antonyms:

stiffness · inelegance

2.   courteous goodwill.
"at least he has the grace to admit his debt to her"

synonyms:

courtesy · courteousness ·

politeness · manners · good manners · mannerliness · civility · decorum · decency · propriety · breeding · respect · respectfulness · consideration · thought · thoughtfulness · tact · tactfulness · diplomacy · etiquette · couth

antonyms:

Effrontery

- (graces)
An attractively polite manner of behaving.

3. "(In Christian belief) the free and unmerited favor of God, as manifested in the salvation of sinners and the bestowal of blessings.
Synonyms:

favor · good will · generosity · kindness · benefaction · beneficence · indulgence

- A divinely given talent or blessing.
"The graces of the Holy Spirit"

4. A period officially allowed for payment of a sum due or for compliance with a law or condition, especially an extended period granted as a special favor.
"Another three days' grace"

Synonyms:

Deferment · deferral ·

postponement · suspension · putting off/back · adjournment · delay · shelving · rescheduling · interruption · arrest · pause · respite · stay · moratorium · reprieve · tabling · continuation · put-off

5.   A short prayer of thanks said before or after a meal.
"Before dinner the Reverend Newman said grace"

Synonyms:

Prayer of thanks · thanksgiving · blessing · benediction

6.   (His Her Your Grace)
Used as forms of description or address for a duke, duchess, or archbishop.

"His Grace, the Duke of Atholl"

7.   (the Graces the Three Graces)
(In Greek mythology) three beautiful goddesses (Aglaia, Thalia, and Euphrosyne) believed to personify and bestow charm, grace, and beauty.

VERB

Grace (verb) · **graces** (third person present) · **graced** (past tense) · **graced** (past participle) · **gracing** (present participle)

8.　　　　　Do honor or credit to (someone or something) by one's presence.
"She bowed out from the sport she has graced for two decades"

Synonyms:

Dignify · distinguish ·

Add distinction to · add dignity to · honor · bestow honor on · favor · enhance · add luster to · magnify · ennoble · glorify · elevate · make lofty · aggrandize · upgrade

Grace has a lot of meanings to it and I would like to add one more. **GRACE IS THE POWER OF GOD IN YOU TO OVERCOME SIN AND DESPAIR.**

Through study and growing in the knowledge of God and our savior Jesus Christ you not only receive more grace but you can be an instrument of grace to others.

Peace

1. "You will keep him in perfect peace, whose mind is stayed on you, because he trusts in you." - **Isaiah 26:3**
2. "Peace I leave with you, my peace I give to you; not as the world gives do I give to you. Let not your heart be troubled, neither let it be afraid." - **John 14:27**
3. "But the wisdom that comes from heaven is first of all pure; then peace-loving, considerate, submissive, full of mercy and good fruit, impartial and sincere." - **James 3:17**
4. "These things I have spoken to you, that in me you may have peace. In the world you will have tribulation; but be of

good cheer, I have overcome the world." - **John 16:33**

5.   "Now may the Lord of peace himself give you peace at all times and in every way? The Lord is with all of you." - **2 Thessalonians 3:16**

6.   "**Be anxious for nothing**, but in everything by prayer and supplication, with thanksgiving, let your requests be made known to God; and the peace of God, which surpasses all understanding, will guard your hearts and minds through Christ Jesus." - **Philippians 4:6-7**

7.   "How beautiful on the mountains are the feet of those who bring good news, who proclaim peace, who bring good tidings, who proclaim salvation, who say to Zion, "Your God reigns!" - **Isaiah 52:7**

8.   "He says, "Be still, and know that I am God; I will be exalted among the nations, I will be exalted in the earth." - **Psalm 46:10**

9.   "The Lord blesses you and keeps you; the Lord makes his face shines on you and is gracious to you; the Lord turns his face

toward you and gives you peace." - **Numbers 6:24-26**

10.   "Make every effort to live in peace with everyone and to be holy; without holiness no one will see the Lord." - **Hebrews 12:14**

11.   "For whoever would love life and see good days must keep their tongue from evil and their lips from deceitful speech. They must turn from evil and do well; they must seek peace and pursue it." - **1 Peter 3:10-11**

12.   "Therefore, since we have been justified through faith, we have peace with God through our Lord Jesus Christ." - **Romans 5:1**

13.   "In peace I will lie down and sleep, for you alone, Lord, make me dwell in safety." - **Psalm 4:8**

14.   "Come to me, all who labor and are heavy laden, and I will give you rest. Take my yoke upon you, and learn from me, for I am gentle and lowly in heart, and you will find rest for your souls. For my yoke is easy,

and my burden is light. "**Matthew 11:28-30**

15.   "Peacemakers who sow in peace reap a harvest of righteousness." - **James 3:18**

16.   "Let the peace of Christ rule in your hearts, since as members of one body you were called to peace. And be thankful." – **Colossians 3:15**

17.   "Finally, brothers, rejoice. Aim for restoration, comfort one another, agree with one another, live in peace; and the God of love and peace will be with you." - **2 Corinthians 13:11**

18.   "Make every effort to keep the unity of the Spirit through the bond of peace." - **Ephesians 4:3**

19.   "For to us a child is born, to us a son is given; and the government shall be upon his shoulder, and his name shall be called Wonderful Counselor, Mighty God, Everlasting Father, Prince of Peace." - **Isaiah 9:6**

20.　　"For to set the mind on the flesh is death, but to set the mind on the Spirit is life and peace." - **Romans 8:6**

A Prayer for Peace

I can't tell you how to find more peace but I can tell you to keep praying:

Jesus, come and be my peace. God, I believe that you know better than me so I am going to leave this in your hands. Help me to look at my present circumstances from your perspective. I want to trust you and rely on your strength to find contentment. I want to share the peace that I find in you with others. When the opportunity comes to speak life and peace to a friend, give me the words and courage to offer: 'Jesus will be your peace.' Amen.

By growing in the knowledge of God and our savior Jesus Christ grace and peace is multiplied to you. Not only to you, but through you, to others. You can be an instrument of grace and peace to all that is within the sphere of your influence. As we continue 2 Peter 1:1-21 you will discover revelation as to why God created you.

3According as his divine power hath given unto us all things that *pertain* unto life and godliness, through the knowledge of him that hath called us to glory and virtue:

Wow!! Powerful, all things are immense and mind boggling.   You mean there isn't anything in life that God through His divine power He hasn't dealt with? What about sickness;

1 Peter 2:24 [24]"He himself bore our sins" in his body on the cross, so that we might die to sins and live for righteousness; "by his wounds you have been healed."

The word have is past tense, we are not trying to get God to do what He has already done and freely given us. Through our knowledge of God and savior Jesus Christ we have to learn how to receive what was already provided to us.

Healing

New King James Version (NKJV)

Jesus said to him, "If you can believe, all things are possible to him who believes." **Mark 9:23 | NKJV**

But when Jesus heard it, He answered him, saying, "Do not be afraid; only believe, and she will be made well." **Luke 8:50 | NKJV**

He heals the brokenhearted
And binds up their wounds. **Psalm 147:3 | NKJV**

Is anyone among you sick? Let him call for the elders of the church, and let them pray over him, anointing him with oil in the name of the Lord. And the prayer of faith will save the sick, and the Lord will raise him up. And if he has committed sins, he will be forgiven. **James 5:14-15 | NKJV**

Then Jesus said to him, "Go your way; your faith has made you well." And immediately he received his sight and followed Jesus on the road. **Mark 10:52 | NKJV**

Heal the sick, cleanse the lepers, raise the dead, cast out demons. Freely you have received, freely give. **Matthew 10:8 | NKJV**

A merry heart does good, like medicine,
But a broken spirit dries the bones.
Proverbs 17:22 | NKJV

Confess your trespasses to one another, and pray for one another, that you may be healed. The effective, fervent prayer of a righteous man avails much. **James 5:16 | NKJV**

If My people who are called by My name will humble themselves, and pray and seek My face, and turn from their wicked ways, then I will hear from heaven, and will forgive their sin and heal their land. **2 Chronicles 7:14 | NKJV**

But He was wounded for our transgressions,
He was bruised for our iniquities;
The chastisement for our peace was upon Him,
And by His stripes we are healed. **Isaiah 53:5 | NKJV**

But to you who fear My name
The Sun of Righteousness shall arise
With healing in His wings;
And you shall go out
And grow fat like stall-fed calves. **Malachi 4:2 | NKJV**

Who Himself bore our sins in His own body

on the tree, that we, having died to sins, might live for righteousness—by whose stripes you were healed. **1 Peter 2:24 | NKJV**

Return and tell Hezekiah the leader of My people, 'Thus says the Lord, the God of David your father: "I have heard your prayer, I have seen your tears; surely I will heal you. On the third day you shall go up to the house of the Lord."' **2 Kings 20:5 | NKJV**

And heal the sick there, and say to them, 'The kingdom of God has come near to you.' **Luke 10:9 | NKJV**

When Jesus heard that, He said to them, "Those who are well have no need of a physician, but those who are sick." **Matthew 9:12 | NKJV**

"If you diligently heed the voice of the Lord your God and do what is right in His sight, give ear to His commandments and keep all His statutes, I will put none of the diseases on you which I have brought on the Egyptians. For I am the Lord who heals you." **Exodus 15:26 | NKJV**

Now He was teaching in one of the synagogues on the Sabbath. And behold, there was a woman who had a spirit of infirmity eighteen years, and was bent over and could in no way raise herself up. But when Jesus saw her, He called her to Him and said to her, "Woman, you are loosed from your infirmity." And He laid His hands on her, and immediately she was made straight, and glorified God.

But the ruler of the synagogue answered with indignation, because Jesus had healed on the Sabbath; and he said to the crowd, "There are six days on which men ought to work; therefore come and be healed on them, and not on the Sabbath day."

The Lord then answered him and said, "Hypocrite! Does not each one of you on the Sabbath loose his ox or donkey from the stall, and lead it away to water it? So ought not this woman, being a daughter of Abraham, whom Satan has bound—think of it—for eighteen years, be loosed from this bond on the Sabbath?" And when He said these things, all His adversaries were put to shame; and all the multitude rejoiced for all the glorious things that were done by Him. **Luke 13:10-17 | NKJV**

The Spirit of the Lord is upon Me,
Because He has anointed Me
To preach the gospel to the poor;
He has sent Me to heal the brokenhearted,
To proclaim liberty to the captives
And recovery of sight to the blind,
To set at liberty those who are oppressed.
Luke 4:18 | NKJV

Heal me, O Lord, and I shall be healed;
Save me, and I shall be saved,
For You are my praise. **Jeremiah**

17:14 | NKJV

The Lord opens the eyes of the blind;
The Lord raises those who are bowed down;
The Lord loves the righteous. **Psalm 146:8 | NKJV**

He sent His word and healed them,
And delivered them from their destructions. **Psalm107:20 | NKJV**

God has provided healing for us so there is only one reason you have not appropriated it to your life and that reason is you. Jesus said to him, "If you can believe, all things are possible to him who believes."

Mark 9:23 | NKJV

Are you of a religious nature and put qualifications and conditions on God healing you? In the scriptures provided I have not noticed the phrase sorry it's not my will to heal you until you learn as lesson.

So far through the knowledge of our God and savior the Lord Jesus Christ we are being transformed from what we were, creatures of the world, lost in sin and corruption and fear to being transformed into people of faith, righteousness, grace, and peace with healing supplied to us. These are not just benefits we receive because we have the knowledge of our God and savior Jesus Christ for our benefit only. Our nature and characters are being changed so these benefits can flow through us to a world that is in crisis. Satan hates the world and continually brings crisis to fulfill his agenda of steal kill and destroy.

What about poverty and lack? Those areas are part of life as well.

PROSPERITY

3 John 1:2 **New King James Version**
Beloved, I pray that you may prosper in all things and be in health, just as your soul prospers.

By growing in the knowledge of God and our savior Jesus Christ our soul is being transformed and will prosper.

Prosper

[ˈpräspər]

VERB

1. Succeed in material terms; be financially successful.
    "His business prospered" · "the nation plans to prosper from free trade with the US"

Synonyms:

do well · get on well · go well · fare well · thrive · flourish · flower · bloom · blossom · burgeon · grow vigorously · shoot up · boom · expand · spread · pick up · improve · come on · succeed · be successful · make it · do all right for oneself · get ahead · progress · make progress · make headway · advance · get on in the world · go up in the world · arrive · fly high · make one's mark · make good · become rich · strike gold/oil · be in clover · go places ·

Go great guns · make the big time · be in the pink · be fine and dandy · be on easy street · live the life of Riley · make good speed

- Flourish physically; grow strong and healthy.

Synonyms:

do well · get on well · go well · fare well · thrive · flourish · flower · bloom · blossom · burgeon · grow vigorously · shoot up · boom · expand · spread · pick up · improve · come on · succeed · be successful · make it · do all right for oneself · get ahead · progress · make progress · make headway · advance · get on in the world · go up in the world · arrive · fly high · make one's mark · make good · become rich · strike gold/oil · be in clover · go places · go great guns · make the big time · be in the pink · be fine and dandy · be on easy street · live the life of Riley · make good speed

•   *archaic*
Make successful.

"God has wonderfully prospered this nation"

God has given us the power to get wealth. That power is found in obedience and faith. It is found in living righteously so that God can pour out His blessing upon us. It is found in us trusting Him in every area of our lives. It is found in us realizing that God is our source. God is your source.

Deuteronomy 8:18 New King James Version

"And you shall remember the LORD your God, for *it is* He who gives you power to get wealth, that He may establish His covenant which He swore to your fathers, as *it is* this day.

2 Corinthians 8:9 [9]For you **know the grace of our LORD Jesus Christ**, that though he was rich, yet for your sake he became poor, so **that** you through his poverty might become rich.

2 Corinthians 9 **The Cheerful Giver**

6But this *I say:* He who sows sparingly will also reap sparingly, and he who sows bountifully will also reap bountifully. **7***So let* each one *give* as he purposes in his heart, not grudgingly or of necessity; for God loves a cheerful giver. **8**And God *is* able to make all grace abound toward you, that you, always having all sufficiency in all *things,* may have abundance for every good work. **9**As it is written:

"He has dispersed abroad,
He has given to the poor;
His righteousness endures forever."

10Now may He who supplies seed to the sower, and bread for food, supply and multiply the seed you have *sown* and increase the fruits of your righteousness, **11**while *you are* enriched in everything for all liberality, which causes thanksgiving through us to God. **12**For the administration of this service not only supplies the needs of the saints, but also is abounding through many thanksgivings to God, **13**while, through the proof of this ministry, they glorify God for the obedience of your confession to the gospel of Christ, and for *your* liberal sharing with them and all *men,* **14**and by their prayer for you, who long for you because of the exceeding grace of God in you. **15**Thanks *be* to God for His indescribable gift!

The reason for financial prosperity is not to indulge in the lust of the flesh and have great possessions that are not necessary for life. Yes deliverance from poverty and enjoy a successful life in every area; Financial, health, emotional, relational, and to be in a financial situation to be a great giver to every good work. To me prosperity is to have enough of God's supply to fulfill God's commands.

The only way to accomplish this is By growing in the knowledge of God and our savior Jesus Christ. By walking in the knowledge of God and our savior Jesus Christ you will not only honor but cause others to praise God because of you.

6 CHANGING NATURES

2 Peter 1:1-21

1Simon Peter, a servant and an apostle of Jesus Christ, to them that have obtained like precious faith with us through the righteousness of God and our Saviour Jesus Christ:

2Grace and peace be multiplied unto you through the knowledge of God, and of Jesus our Lord,

3According as his divine power hath given unto us all things that *pertain* unto life and godliness, through the knowledge of him that hath called us to glory and virtue:

4Whereby are given unto us exceeding great and precious promises: that by these ye might be partakers of the divine nature, having escaped the corruption that is in the world through lust.

5And beside this, giving all diligence, add to your faith virtue; and to virtue knowledge;

6And to knowledge temperance; and to temperance patience; and to patience godliness;

7And to godliness brotherly kindness; and to brotherly kindness charity.

8For if these things be in you, and abound, they make *you that ye shall* neither *be* barren nor unfruitful in the knowledge of our Lord Jesus Christ.

9But he that lacketh these things is blind, and cannot see afar off, and hath forgotten that he was purged from his old sins.

10Wherefore the rather, brethren, give diligence to make your calling and election sure: for if ye do these things, ye shall never fall:

11For so an entrance shall be ministered unto you abundantly into the everlasting kingdom of our Lord and Saviour Jesus Christ.

12Wherefore I will not be negligent to put you always in remembrance of these things, though ye know *them,* and be established in the present truth.

13Yea, I think it meet, as long as I am in this tabernacle, to stir you up by putting *you* in remembrance;

14Knowing that shortly I must put off *this* my tabernacle, even as our Lord Jesus Christ hath shewed me.

15Moreover I will endeavour that ye may be able after my decease to have these things always in remembrance.

16For we have not followed cunningly devised fables, when we made known unto you the power and coming of our Lord Jesus Christ, but were eyewitnesses of his majesty.

17He received honor and glory from God the Father when the voice came to him from the Majestic Glory, saying, "This is my Son, whom I love; with him I am well pleased."

18And this voice which came from heaven we heard, when we were with him in the holy mount.

19We have also a more sure word of prophecy; whereunto ye do well that ye

take heed, as unto a light that shineth in a dark place, until the day dawn, and the day star arise in your hearts:

20Knowing this first, that no prophecy of the scripture is of any private interpretation.

21For the prophecy came not in old time by the will of man: but holy men of God spake *as they were* moved by the Holy Ghost.

We are going to look at verse 4-8 in this section

4Whereby are given unto us exceeding great and precious promises: that by these ye might be partakers of the divine nature, having escaped the corruption that is in the world through lust. **5**And beside this, giving all diligence, add to your faith virtue; and to virtue knowledge;

6And to knowledge temperance; and to temperance patience; and to patience godliness;

7And to godliness brotherly kindness; and to brotherly kindness charity.

8For if these things be in you, and abound, they make *you that ye*
shall neither *be* barren nor unfruitful in the knowledge of our Lord Jesus Christ.

When mankind fell in the Garden of Eden we lost our nature to naturally commune with God and inherited a nature of fear and unbelief. **Genesis 3:8 New King James Version**
And they heard the sound of the LORD God walking in the garden in the cool of the day, and Adam and his wife hid themselves from the presence of the LORD God among the trees of the garden.

Revelation 6:15
Then the kings of the earth, the nobles, the commanders, the rich, the mighty, and every slave and free man, hid in the caves and among the rocks of the mountains.

God's intent was never to be separated from mankind. **Leviticus 26:12** I will walk among you and be your God, and you will be My people.

Through His promises God has given us the ability to put on the divine nature again and fellowship with Him.

1 Corinthians 2:16 - For who hath known the mind of the Lord, that he may instruct him? But we have the mind of Christ.

Romans 12:2 - And be not conformed to this world: but be ye transformed by the renewing of your mind, that ye may prove what [is] that good, and acceptable, and perfect, will of God.

1 Corinthians 2:14-16 - But the natural man receiveth not the things of the Spirit of God: for they are foolishness unto him: neither can he know [them], because they are spiritually discerned.

Philippians 2:5 - Let this mind be in you, which was also in Christ Jesus:

1 Corinthians 2:13-16 - Which things also we speak, not in the words which man's wisdom teacheth, but which the Holy Ghost teacheth; comparing spiritual things with spiritual.

2 Timothy 1:7 - For God hath not given us the spirit of fear; but of power, and of love, and of a sound mind.

1 Peter 1:13 - Wherefore gird up the loins of your mind, be sober, and hope to the end for the grace that is to be brought unto you at the revelation of Jesus Christ;

Philippians 2:5-11 - Let this mind be in you, which was also in Christ Jesus:

1 Peter 4:17 - For the time [is come] that judgment must begin at the house of God: and if [it] first [begin] at us, what shall the end [be] of them that obey not the gospel of God?

1 Peter 1:3 - Blessed [be] the God and Father of our Lord Jesus Christ, which according to his abundant mercy hath begotten us again unto a lively hope by the resurrection of Jesus Christ from the dead,

John 5:30 - I can of mine own self do nothing: as I hear, I judge: and my judgment is just; because I seek not mine own will, but the will of the Father which hath sent me.

Ephesians 5:1 - Be ye therefore followers of

God, as dear children;

1 John 2:6 - He that saith he abideth in him ought himself also so to walk, even as he walked.

Romans 8:1-39 - [There is] therefore now no condemnation to them which are in Christ Jesus, who walk not after the flesh, but after the Spirit.

Philippians 4:8 - Finally, brethren, whatsoever things are true, whatsoever things [are] honest, whatsoever things [are] just, whatsoever things [are] pure, whatsoever things [are] lovely, whatsoever things [are] of good report; if [there be] any virtue, and if [there be] any praise, think on these things.

James 1:27 - Pure religion and undefiled

before God and the Father is this, To visit the fatherless and widows in their affliction, [and] to keep himself unspotted from the world.

2 Peter 1: 5 And beside this, giving all diligence, add to your faith virtue; and to virtue knowledge;
6And to knowledge temperance; and to temperance patience; and to patience godliness;
7And to godliness brotherly kindness; and to brotherly kindness charity.
8For if these things be in you, and abound, they make *you that ye*
shall neither *be* barren nor unfruitful in the knowledge of our Lord Jesus Christ.

When you read verse 5 to 8 you are actually reading the nature of God as shown in Galatians 5:22-23

New King James Version

[22] But the fruit of the Spirit is love, joy, peace, longsuffering,

kindness, goodness, faithfulness, [23] gentlene
ss,

self-control. Against such there is no law.
The question is how do you add these
attributes to your life? **Proverbs 18:21 New
King James Version**
Death and life *are* in the power of the
tongue, And those who love it will eat its
fruit.

We are created in God's image and likeness
and when He speaks a word it comes to
pass. Isaiah 55:11, which says, "So **shall my
word be that goes forth out of my mouth**:
it shall not return unto me void, but it shall
accomplish that which I please, and it shall
prosper in the thing whereto I sent it."
so if we are created in the image and
likeness of God and his words accomplish
the thing it was sent to do, wouldn't it
reason out to say our words have the same
abilities?

Mark 9:23 New King James Version

Jesus said to him, "If you can believe, all things *are* possible to him who believes."

Through faith in God's word and the power of the holy Spirit we personalize the scriptures and speak them over ourselves. Speak the fruit of the spirit over yourself in personal application **I AM LOVE; I AM JOY; I AM PEACE; I AM LONGSUFFERING; I AM KINDNESS; I AM GOODNESS; I AM FAITHFULNESS; I AM GENTLENESS.** As you speak these over your life you will see a change in your thinking and nature especially in how you treat other people.

Some people may be adventurous and confess the scripture over themselves one or two times then complain nothing happened. There is a reason **2 Peter 1: 5**And beside this, giving all **diligence,** add to your faith virtue; and to virtue knowledge.

The word diligence is here.

diligence

[ˈdiləjəns]

NOUN

diligence *(noun)*

1.   careful and persistent work or effort.
   "few party members challenge his
   diligence as an MP"

   synonyms:

   conscientiousness · assiduousness · assidui
   ty · industriousness · rigor · rigorousness ·
   punctiliousness · meticulousness ·

   carefulness · thoroughness · sedulousness ·
    attentiveness ·

   heedfulness · earnestness · intentness · stu
   diousness ·

   constancy · perseverance · persistence · te
   nacity · pertinacity · zeal · zealousness · de
   dication · commitment · tirelessness ·

indefatigability · doggedness · industry · ha rdwork · application · effort · concentration · care · attention · laboriousness ·

continuance · perseveration

antonyms:

laziness · carelessness

When you start on your journey to be in fellowship with God it's a lifelong journey. Now the just shall live by faith; But if anyone draws back, My soul has no pleasure in him – Hebrews 10:38 (NKJV).
"For thus says the LORD: 'You shall not see wind, nor shall you see rain; yet that valley shall be filled with water, so that you, your cattle, and your animals may drink – II Kings 3:17 (NKJV).
Many Christians start off in **faith**, but down the line before they see their desired result they draw back on their faith. Sadly, they lose their blessings when they do so. God says He has no pleasure in anyone who draws back on his or her faith. This means

that God has pleasure in anyone who exercises his faith till he receives his desires, without faith it is impossible to please God (Hebrews 11:6).

The just shall live by faith. Our Christian walk is a walk of faith and faith is acting on God's word. We are to hold unto that word of God till we receive our desired result knowing who said it and what He is capable of doing. God wants us to trust in His words. The Lord says what He means and means what He says. He watches over His word to perform it (Jeremiah 1:12).

Christians draw back on their faith because their focus moved from the word of God to issues on ground, and at that moment they doubted the ability of the word of the Lord to deliver. In other words, they doubted the Master's ability to do as He had said. You are to stand on God's word till you see it manifested physically. The word of the Lord never fails, every declared word of God will not return to Him without accomplishing the purpose for which He sent it (Isaiah 55:11).

Faith connects you to God, but anytime you draw back on your faith, you disconnect from God and it doesn't please Him. When Peter acted on Jesus' word "come" he connected to God but when he removed his eyes from Jesus and focused on the **storm** (the intensity of the challenge on ground) he disconnected from God and started sinking; Jesus was not pleased with him because he doubted (Matthew 14:28-32).

Abraham, on the other hand, believed the Lord till the end when he obeyed and went on to sacrifice his son Isaac. God had told him that in Isaac his seed shall be called, yet God asked him to sacrifice Isaac. He concluded that God was able to raise Isaac up again even from the dead in order to fulfill His promise to him (Genesis 22:1-19, Hebrews 11:17-9). He didn't doubt God's word at all. At the end God swore a blessing upon him which his children the Israelites, generations after him, are still enjoying till date.

Kenneth E. Hagin in one of his books "Mountain Moving Faith" shared a testimony of how he believed that God had healed his face according to His word but there was no physical manifestation of it. People who heard his testimony and could still see his face unchanged tried to persuade him to believe that he wasn't healed. He refused to doubt in spite of what the people were seeing and saying. He held unto the Lord's words and by the next day, his face had conformed to the word of God, totally made whole.

In conclusion, if you believe God to do something for you based on what He had said, don't draw back on your faith no matter what your eyes and ears are seeing and hearing. Though you may not see wind nor rain, be rest assured that it shall be even as the Lord had said, the valley shall be full of water (2 Kings 3:17). You have need of faith and patience that after you have done the will of God, you might receive the promise (Hebrews 10:36). Therefore, receive grace today never to draw back on your faith in Jesus name. https://stepswithgod.com/draw-faith/

We were created in the God class of being to have fellowship with the creator of all things. Lucifer wanted to be like God but God created mankind to be like Him for a purpose not a need but a want. He wanted a creation like himself to fellowship with and show love to and His goodness. That creation has the ability to choose to show the God kind of Love (AGAPE) unconditional love back to their creator. To love God not for what they can get from Him but to love Him for himself. This kind of fellowship fulfills man's heart and pleases God.

Ephesians 2:7-10 [7] that in the ages to come He might show the exceeding riches of His grace in *His* kindness toward us in Christ Jesus. [8] For by grace you have been saved through faith, and that not of yourselves; *it is* the gift of God, [9] not of works, lest anyone should boast. [10] For we are His workmanship, created in Christ Jesus for good works, which God prepared beforehand that we should walk in them.

You were created on purpose and for purpose. Don't let anyone rob you of your God given purpose, as you fellowship with God which is your main purpose you will discover the destiny for your life

7 YOUR CALLING

2 Peter 1:1-21

1Simon Peter, a servant and an apostle of Jesus Christ, to them that have obtained like precious faith with us through the righteousness of God and our Saviour Jesus Christ:

2Grace and peace be multiplied unto you through the knowledge of God, and of Jesus our Lord,

3According as his divine power hath given unto us all things that *pertain* unto life and godliness, through the knowledge of him that hath called us to glory and virtue:

4Whereby are given unto us exceeding great and precious promises: that by these ye might be partakers of the divine nature, having escaped the corruption that is in the world through lust.

5And beside this, giving all diligence, add to your faith virtue; and to virtue knowledge;

6And to knowledge temperance; and to temperance patience; and to patience godliness;

7And to godliness brotherly kindness; and to brotherly kindness charity.

8For if these things be in you, and abound, they make *you that ye*

shall neither *be* barren nor unfruitful in the knowledge of our Lord Jesus Christ.

9But he that lacketh these things is blind, and cannot see afar off, and hath forgotten that he was purged from his old sins.

10Wherefore the rather, brethren, give diligence to make your calling and election sure: for if ye do these things, ye shall never fall:

11For so an entrance shall be ministered unto you abundantly into the everlasting kingdom of our Lord and Saviour Jesus Christ.

12Wherefore I will not be negligent to put you always in remembrance of these things, though ye know *them*, and be established in the present truth.

13Yea, I think it meet, as long as I am in this tabernacle, to stir you up by putting *you* in remembrance;

14Knowing that shortly I must put off *this* my tabernacle, even as our Lord Jesus Christ hath shewed me.

15Moreover I will endeavour that ye may be able after my decease to have these things always in remembrance.

16For we have not followed cunningly devised fables, when we made known unto you the power and coming of our Lord Jesus Christ, but were eyewitnesses of his majesty.

 17He received honor and glory from God the Father when the voice came to him from the Majestic Glory, saying, "This is my Son, whom I love; with him I am well pleased."

18And this voice which came from heaven we heard, when we were with him in the holy mount.

19We have also a more sure word of prophecy; whereunto ye do well that ye

take heed, as unto a light that shineth in a dark place, until the day dawn, and the day star arise in your hearts:

20Knowing this first, that no prophecy of the scripture is of any private interpretation.

I want to look at the area of calling. Many Christian think many are called but few are chosen and that applies to the fivefold ministry.

Matthew 22 14 New King James Version

"For many are called, but few *are* chosen."

1 Peter 2:9 New King James Version

⁹ But you *are* a chosen generation, a royal priesthood, a holy nation, His own special people, that you may proclaim the praises of Him who called you out of darkness into His marvelous light;

Acts 17:30 New King James Version

Truly, these times of ignorance God overlooked, but now commands all men everywhere to repent,

I believe we are the ones who do the choosing. God commands us to repent and we choose to obey. God calls us into fellowship and we choose to obey. Through fellowship with the Holy Spirit we make choices every day. Our choices are either obedience to blessings or selfishness to trouble. **Deuteronomy 11:26-28 New King James Version**

26 "Behold, I set before you today a blessing and a curse: 27 the blessing, if you obey the commandments of the LORD your God which I command you today; 28 and the curse, if you do not obey the commandments of the LORD your God, but turn aside from the way which I command you today, to go after other gods which you have not known.

Other gods may not be the stone idols in days of old instead something you have an attachment to more intense than your relationship with the Holy Spirit.

10Wherefore the rather, brethren, give diligence to make your calling and election sure: for if ye do these things, ye shall never fall:

I believe Ephesians 4 has the answer to the believers calling.

Ephesians 4

New King James Version

Walk in Unity

4 I, therefore, the prisoner of the Lord, beseech you to walk worthy of the calling with which you were called, [2] with all lowliness and gentleness, with longsuffering, bearing with one another in love, [3] endeavoring to keep the unity of the Spirit in the bond of peace. [4] *There is* one body and one Spirit, just as you were called in one hope of your calling; [5] one Lord, one faith, one baptism; [6] one God and Father of all, who *is* above all, and through all, and in you all.

Spiritual Gifts

7 But to each one of us grace was given according to the measure of Christ's gift. **8** Therefore He says:

"When He ascended on high,
He led captivity captive,
and gave gifts to men."

9 (Now this, "He ascended"—what does it mean but that He also first descended into the lower parts of the earth? **10** He who descended is also the One who ascended far above all the heavens, that He might fill all things.)

11 And He Himself gave some *to be* apostles, some prophets, some evangelists, and some pastors and teachers, **12** for the equipping of the saints for the work of ministry, for the edifying of the body of Christ, **13** till we all come to the unity of the faith and of the knowledge of the Son of God, to a perfect man, to the measure of the stature of the fullness of Christ; [14] that we should no longer be children, tossed to and fro and carried about with every wind of doctrine, by the trickery of men, in the cunning craftiness of deceitful plotting, [15] but, speaking the truth in love, may grow up in all things into Him who is the head—Christ— [16] from whom the whole body, joined and knit together by what every joint supplies, according to the effective working by which every part does its share, causes growth of the body for the edifying of itself in love.

The New Man

[17] This I say, therefore, and testify in the Lord, that you should no longer walk as the rest of the Gentiles walk, in the futility of their mind, [18] having their understanding darkened, being alienated from the life of God, because of the ignorance that is in them, because of the blindness of their

heart; ¹⁹ who, being past feeling, have given themselves over to lewdness, to work all uncleanness with greediness.

²⁰ But you have not so learned Christ, ²¹ if indeed you have heard Him and have been taught by Him, as the truth is in Jesus: ²² that you put off, concerning your former conduct, the old man which grows corrupt according to the deceitful lusts, ²³ and be renewed in the spirit of your mind, ²⁴ and that you put on the new man which was created according to God, in true righteousness and holiness.

Do Not Grieve the Spirit

²⁵ Therefore, putting away lying, "*Let* each one *of you* speak truth with his neighbor," for we are members of one another. ²⁶ "Be angry, and do not sin": do not let the sun go down on your wrath, ²⁷ nor give place to the devil. ²⁸ Let him who stole steal no longer, but rather let him labor, working with *his* hands what is

good, that he may have something to give him who has need. **29** Let no corrupt word proceed out of your mouth, but what is good for necessary edification, that it may impart grace to the hearers. **30** And do not grieve the Holy Spirit of God, by whom you were sealed for the day of redemption. **31** Let all bitterness, wrath, anger, clamor, and evil speaking be put away from you, with all malice. **32** And be kind to one another, tender-hearted, forgiving one another, even as God in Christ forgave you.

Verse 11 and 12 tell the purpose of the fivefold ministry. **11** And He Himself gave some *to be* apostles, some prophets, some evangelists, and some pastors and teachers, **12 for the equipping of the saints for the work of ministry, for the edifying of the body of Christ,**

Your calling is to be a minister within the sphere of influence God has entrusted you to. Be a witness of the Glory of God and build your fellow believers in love. When we walk as people who are in relationship with the Holy Spirit and unconditional love towards the Body of Christ we will be a witness to the world of God's goodness.

John 13:35 New King James Version

By this all will know that you are My disciples, if you have love for one another."

8 EPILOGUE

We deal with the question why did God create me? We go to religious leaders only to get an unsatisfactory answer or if you have talents they want in their church you get Self-motivated answers. A strong relationship with the Holy Spirit will reveal who you are and your purpose. One reason I found why some religious leaders give you demeaning answers is because they feel threatened by the call on your life. They don't want to have to deal with someone who in their mind is greater than themselves. Nevertheless it's not about greatness or fame or riches, it's about fellowship with the Holy Spirit and fulfilling your destiny. On that day I want to hear from Jesus **"WELL DONE ENTER INTO THE JOY OF THE LORD**

9 ABOUT THE AUTHOR

William carries the anointing of a prophet and psalmist. He is also a Bible teacher, author and international speaker. He operates in all of the Spiritual gifts. He uses the gifts as the Holy Spirit wills. One of William's great desires is to lead others to Christ and to follow Holy Spirit wherever He leads.

YOU CAN VISIT MY WEBSITE
WWW.PSALMISTWILLIAM.CA
FOR ENCOURAGING PSALMS AND TO BUY OTHER BOOKS I HAVE WRITTEN